I love you!
Thanks for being the best
father I could ever
hope for on my children!
—me

OTHER GIFTBOOKS IN THIS SERIES

baby boy!   *mum*   *happy day!*
baby girl!   *smile*   *hope! dream!*
friend   *love*

Printed simultaneously in 2004 by Helen Exley Giftbooks
in Great Britain and Helen Exley Giftbooks LLC in the USA.

12 11 10 9 8 7 6 5 4 3 2

Illustrations © Joanna Kidney 2004
Copyright © Helen Exley 2004
Text copyright – see page 94
The moral right of the author has been asserted.

ISBN 1-86187-763-3

Edited by Helen Exley
Pictures by Joanna Kidney

Printed in China

Helen Exley Giftbooks, 16 Chalk Hill, Watford, Herts WD19 4BG, UK.
Helen Exley Giftbooks LLC, 185 Main Street, Spencer MA 01562, USA.
www.helenexleygiftbooks.com

A HELEN EXLEY GIFTBOOK

dad

PICTURES BY JOANNA KIDNEY

Your dad is there to add sparkle

and surprise to your childhood.

SIÂN E. MORGAN, B.1973

Dad is always on your side,
cheering for you.
It doesn't matter a bit
whether you're first or last,
he's your top supporter.

MARGOT THOMSON

One little word from dad,
one simple compliment
– that is all it takes to completely

uplift your heart and brighten your spirit.

STUART MACFARLANE, B.1953

The greatest gift a parent
can ever give to a child,
my father gave to us
time and time again
– himself.

HANA ALI,
FROM "MORE THAN A HERO"

A MILLION WORDS,
UNSPOKEN,
TELL THE LOVE
WE HAVE FOR DAD.

STUART AND LINDA MACFARLANE

TO A YOUNG CHILD,
THE FATHER IS A GIANT
FROM WHOSE SHOULDERS
YOU CAN SEE FOREVER.

PERRY GARFINKEL

...my father would pick me up
and hold me high in the air.
He dominated my life as long as he lived,
and was the love of my life.

ELEANOR ROOSEVELT
(1884–1962)

Thank you for the memories,
the joys you crafted out of love,
the small adventures
you've devised for me,
the companionship
that we shared.

PAM BROWN, B.1928

DAD IS THE TOPS.
He's your best ball-catcher,
    your best thrower-up-into-the-air,

your best pretend king

and the best funny face-maker.

RICHARD ALAN

Dad: A man who takes
a second job
    to subsidize
    the toy industry.

STUART AND LINDA MACFARLANE

TO SEE PERFECT JOY,
WATCH A LITTLE CHILD RUNNING,
ARMS OUTSTRETCHED,
TO THOSE
OF ITS RETURNING DAD.

PAM BROWN, B.1928

He gives everything
so unselfishly
– his love, his time
and most importantly his tender,
caring support
in everything I do.

LINDA MACFARLANE, B.1953

Parents are generally
wonderful people
who give all their hearts and energy
to the little people
they have called into the universe.

JOHN O'DONOHUE,
FROM "ETERNAL ECHOES"

When the weather's cold
and the day is dreary,
to see a dad
and his little child together,
lost in love for one another,
brings the sun back to the sky.

PAM BROWN, B.1928

Dads take building sandcastles
very seriously,
it has to be a masterpiece
big enough to live in
and it has to be
the best one on the beach.

PASCAL UMBERT

"Up" she says – and up she comes,
safe to his shoulder,
wrapped in his arms,
delighting in the loving nonsense he is saying.
"Down" she says,
and slithers to the floor,
to hold his hand fast,
and stomp along beside him.
"Oops" she says
– falls flat and waits for rescue.
"Sing" she says, and dances to his tune.

PAM BROWN, B.1928

I remember

the sound of his laughter.

ELLEN LAWRENCE, FROM "OUT OF THE SHADOWS"
IN "A LONG HOT SOAK"

New dads carry shopping bags,
push buggies, wipe bottoms,
load washing machines
and festoon themselves with babies.
They take their reward
in smiles and kisses.

PAM BROWN, B.1928

The seaside is a place
to sit on fathers,
        to take them paddling,
to drag them off for ice-cream,
to bury bits of them in sand.
    To ask for a little carry to the car.
And to demand they stop –
            most urgently
    – as you have to find a loo.

PAM BROWN, B.1928

Dad's love,

Warmth on a winter's day,

    Gentle when times are hard,

Funny when I feel down,

    Firm when I'm being ghastly,

    ...everything I ever need.

LINDA MACFARLANE, B.1953

Dads take their children's hands
and lead them into the wider world –
        showing them the things they loved
– trees and moors and rivers,
                castles and museums.
    And the children return his gifts
a thousand-fold
            – showing him the things
that he had long forgotten.

PAM BROWN, B.1928

There is something ultimate
in a father's love,
         something that cannot fail,
something to be believed
         against the whole world.
We almost attribute practical
omnipotence to our father
         in the days of our childhood.

FREDERICK WILLIAM FABER (1814–1863)

The people to whom we owe the most
never remind us of our debts.
They send no bills
and they demand no settlement...
I am thinking
of one of the greatest of my own debts
– the one to my father.

EDGAR A. GUEST (1881–1959),
FROM "MOMENTS WITH FATHER"

Together,
they explore the toy shop window.
Together, they admire the digger shifting dirt.
Together, they rejoice in ducks
and cats and cherry blossom.
"Home" she says
– and off they go together,
to toast and sponge cakes
– and a cuddle in the big armchair.

PAM BROWN, B.1928

My father once turned up...
I'd just taken a hat trick
and as I turned, I saw him.
He looked up at me
and gently applauded.
We didn't speak
but that gesture was enough.

HENRY KELLY,
FROM "WOMEN & HOME" DECEMBER 1994

My father had the gift
of making me believe,
and of believing himself,
that there is always a new adventure,
something, waiting to be discovered,
if we can only find the time
to look for it,
and the courage to jump.

KUKI GALLMAN,
FROM "I DREAMED OF AFRICA"

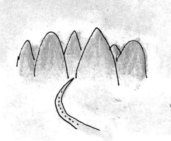

He was protective, strong,
and I could fall asleep knowing
that I would wake up
safe and sound.

TONY PARSON, FROM "FATHER'S DAY"

All about him was safe.

NAOMI MITCHISON
(1897–1999)

A FATHER'S LOVE
FOR HIS DAUGHTER
IS AS SOFT AS A SNOWFLAKE
YET AS STRONG
AS STEEL.

STUART AND LINDA MACFARLANE

A father is
a man whose days
   are illuminated
by his children's
        smiles.

PAM BROWN, B.1928

You are my childhood.
Peaceful days on the sands,
    paddling in the pools,
happiness,
    sandcastles,
counting shells...
    my memories seem
like a wonderful dream,
    they mean so much.

HELEN THOMSON, B.1943

It's only when you grow up,
and step back from him,
or leave him for your own career
and your own home
– it's only then that you can measure
his greatness and fully appreciate it.

MARGARET TRUMAN

How do you thank someone
for love beyond words?
For the sense
that I'd trust you with my life;
and that you are one

of the two or three people
that I can truly trust;
that cares, understands
and offers (unconditionally)
to help me in my life.

DALTON EXLEY

You're part of whatever I do or achieve –
because you taught me
and encouraged me and stood by me.
Always.

CHARLOTTE GRAY, B.1937

Daddy was my rock, my anchor,
the root of my strength.

ANN-MARGARET, FROM "MY STORY"

Dear Dad,
it is for your quirks and foibles

that your children cherish you
— not for your successes.

CHARLOTTE GRAY B.1937

To me the important things
about my father
are the good things.
His energy, his enthusiasm,
his sense of loyalty, his love of family.

I don't see the world
from the same perspective that he does,
but even now
there are very few important situations
that arise where I don't ask myself
how he would handle
the situation.

PEG PALMER WEARS

Thanks, Dad, for embarrassing me by,

Collecting me from the school dance,

Cheering so loudly

when I graduated from college,

Insisting on checking out all my boyfriends.

Now I understand

and I'm proud

that you loved me that much.

LINDA MACFARLANE, B.1953

Children hold their dads
forever in their hearts
   – not for their good looks or brilliance –
but for a balding patch, a trick of speech.
      For mild eccentricities.
      Small adventures, promises kept.
   For being their own,
                  dear, special dad.

PAMELA DUGDALE

All the shared hopes and fears,
all the times of joy
and sorrow entwine
like a vine binding parent and child
together in a mutual love
that lasts eternally.

STUART AND LINDA MACFARLANE

Through you I learned
how great life can be,
how the simple things in life
are really the most important
and how you treat other people
is really all that matters.

LISA SCULLY-O'GRADY

You worship him as your defender, your hero, your big brave Dad.

Later, you discover he's really

a quieter, shorter more ordinary man
– and your lifelong friend.

MARGOT THOMSON

A dad's love
is a child's most precious belonging.

It is unconditional, total,
and lasts for ever
and ever and ever.

STUART AND LINDA MACFARLANE

A happy childhood
can't be cured.
Mine'll hang
around my neck
like a rainbow,

AUTHOR UNKNOWN

A good father
leaves so many joyful, enduring memories
in his child's mind
like a bank of emotional strengths
that can be drawn on through
the testing years ahead.

MARGOT THOMSON

Did I ever say, "Thank you",
For putting up with all my nonsense?
For loving me?
For teaching me to ride my bike?
For holding me?
For all those bedtime stories?
For being proud of me?
For these
and a million, million other things,
"Thanks Dad."

STUART MACFARLANE, B.1953

And you there – and so...
all safe.
　　My shield from all harm.
Giving me certainty
　　　　– that safe, still place
　　to which I can always turn.

PAM BROWN, B.1928

Helen Exley runs her own publishing company which sells giftbooks in more than seventy countries. She had always wanted to do a little book on smiles, and had been collecting the quotations for many years, but always felt that the available illustrations just weren't quite right. Then Helen fell in love with Joanna Kidney's happy, bright pictures and knew immediately they had the feel she was looking for. She asked Joanna to work on *smile*, and then to go on to contribute the art for four more books: *friend*, *happy day!*, *love* and *hope! dream!* We are now publishing five more books in this series, *dad*, *mum*, *baby boy!*, *baby girl!* and *wedding*.

Joanna Kidney lives in County Wicklow in Ireland. She juggles her time between working on various illustration projects and producing her own art for shows and exhibitions. Her whole range of greeting cards, *Joanna's Pearlies* – some of which appear in this book – won the prestigious 2001 Henries oscar for 'best fun or graphic range'.

Text Copyright: The publishers are grateful for permission to reproduce copyright material. Whilst every reasonable effort has been made to trace copyright holders, the publishers would be pleased to hear from any not here acknowledged. PEG PALMER WEARS: From *Arnold Palmer: A Personal Journey*, published by Collins Publishers. PAM BROWN, PAMELA DUGDALE, DALTON EXLEY, LISA SCULLY-O'GRADY, CHARLOTTE GRAY, SIÂN E. MORGAN, HELEN THOMSON, MARGOT THOMSON, STUART AND LINDA MACFARLANE, PASCAL UMBERT © HELEN EXLEY 2004.